Grade 1

Scott Foresman

Strategic Intervention Decodable Readers

Editorial Offices: Glenview, Illinois • Parsippany, New Jersey • New York, New York
Sales Offices: Needham, Massachusetts • Duluth, Georgia • Glenview, Illinois
Coppell, Texas • Sacramento, California • Mesa, Arizona

ISBN: 0-328-14507-6

8 9 10 V084 14 13 12 11 10 09 08

Contents

Strategic Intervention
Decodable Reader 1

Mack and Tack

Written by Sally Hinkley
Illustrated by Dan Vick

Phonics Skills

Short a			Final -ck	
Mack	sat	pat	Mack	sack
had	hat	sack	Tack	
Tack	ran	can		
nab				

Tack ran.
Mack ran.
Can Mack nab Tack?

8

Mack sat.
Pat Mack.

2

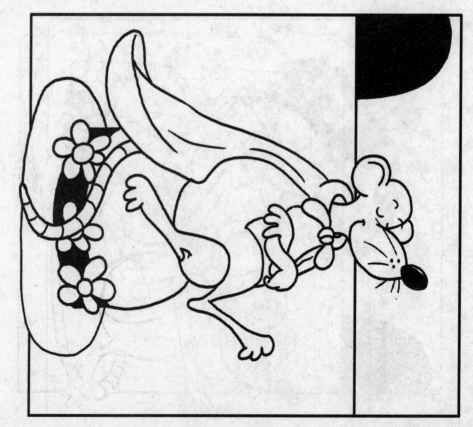

Tack sat on the hat.

7

Mack had a hat.
Mack had a sack.

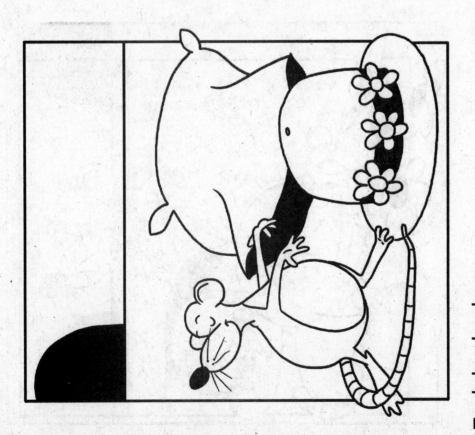

Tack had a hat.
Tack had a sack.

Mack sat in the sack.

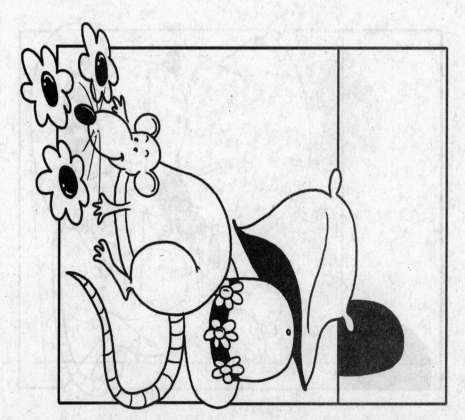

Tack sat.
Pat Tack.

Strategic Intervention Decodable Reader 2

Kim Did!

Written by Cory Stell

Illustrated by Jan Lever

Phonics Skills

Short i		Final -x	
did	it	mix	fix
Kim	sit		
tip	mix		
pin	fix		

Did Kim fix it?
Kim and Sam did!

8

Did Sam see it?
Kim did!

Did Kim pin it?
Kim did!

Did Kim take it?
Kim did!

Did Kim mix it up?
Kim did!

Did Kim sit on it?
Kim did!

4

Did Kim tip it?
Kim did!

5

Rob did.
Dot did.
Dad did.
Mom did not.

On Top

Written by Bill Pots
Illustrated by Randy Gunn

Phonics Skills

Short o			Plural -s /s/, /z/	
got	on	rocks	rocks	pots
Dot	not	Rob		
Mom	box	pots		

Dad got on the rocks.

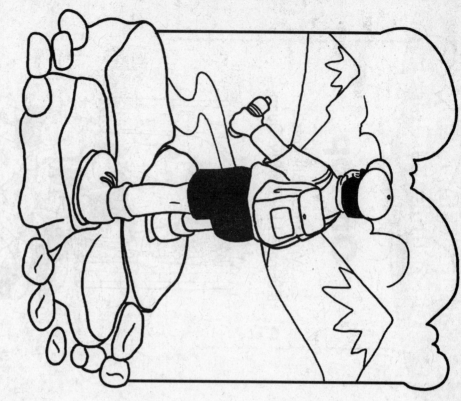

Dad can use pots.
Mom can not.

Dot did not.
Rob did not.

Dot and Rob help get pots.

Dot got on the rocks.

4

Mom got on the box.

5

Can We Nap?

Written by Judy Wolfe
Illustrated by Vince DePinto

Phonics Skills

Inflected Ending -s		Inflected Ending -ing
rocks	naps	rocking kicking
		picking ticking

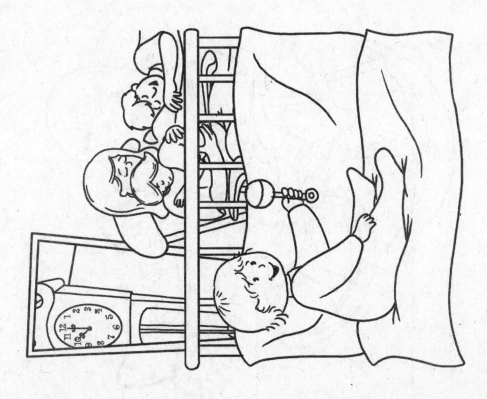

Tick! Tock!
It is ticking.

8

Take a nap, Nan.

Mom naps.
Dad naps.
Sam naps.
Can Nan nap?

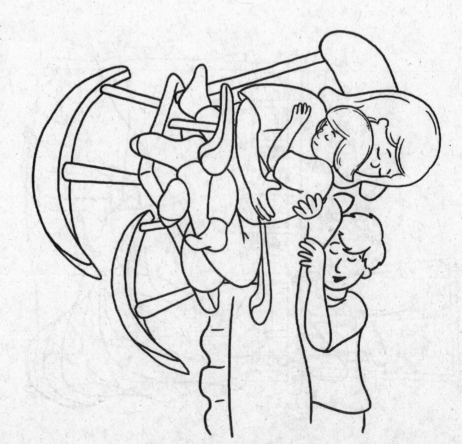

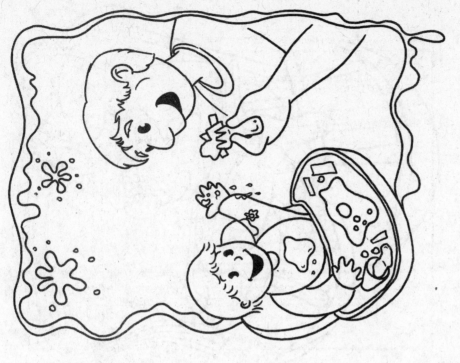

Dad and Nan eat.
Nan has a bib.

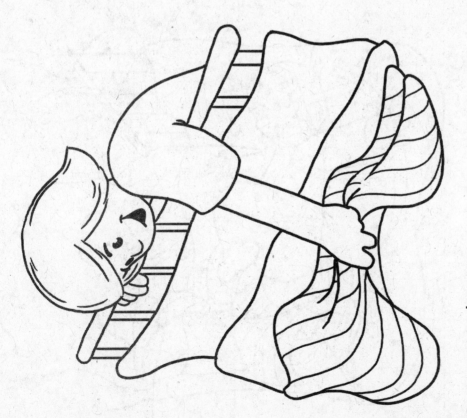

Sam is picking it up.

6

Mom is rocking Nan.
Mom rocks her.

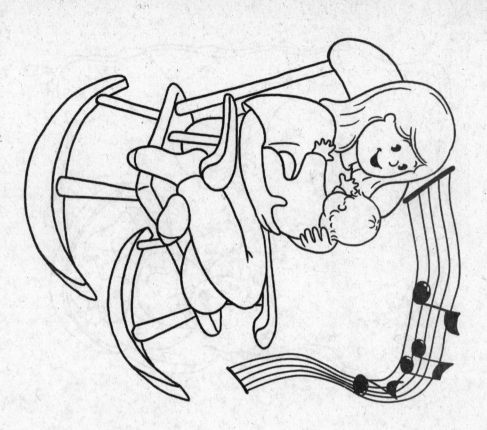

4

Nan is kicking.

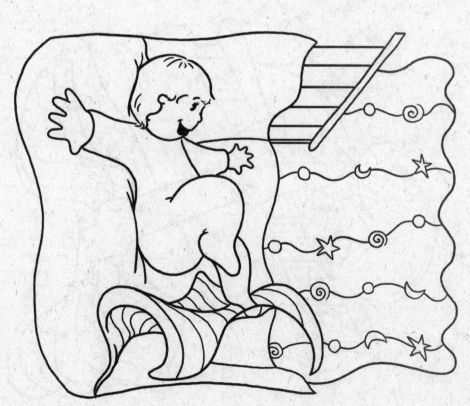

5

Strategic Intervention Decodable Reader 5

The Sleds

Written by Alphie Heart

Illustrated by Joy Stevenson

Phonics Skills

Short e		Consonant Blends (CCVC)	
Peg	sled	sled	sleds
Meg	red	Fred	
sleds	Fred		
get			
Ken			
Ned			

Get on your sleds!
Get Ned.
Get Fred.

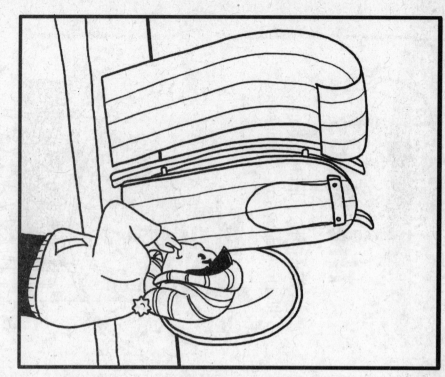

Peg can get a sled.

Ken can get a red sled.

Peg can get a small sled.

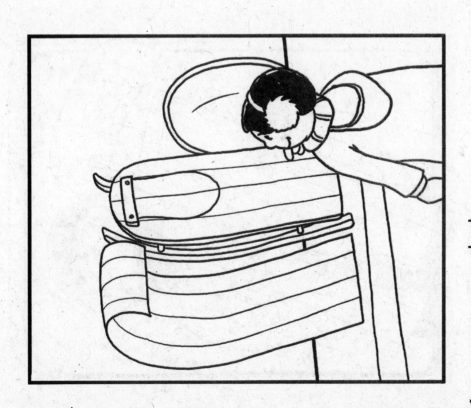

Ken can get a sled.

6

Meg can get a sled.

Meg can get a big sled.

Strategic Intervention
Decodable Reader 6

Cub and Mom

Written by Joyce Burk
Illustrated by David Stoll

Phonics Skills

Short u		Consonant Blends (CVCC)	
Cub	fun	pond	bent
up	nut	plant	and
nuts	dug	must	rest
mud	must		

Cub and Mom can nap at home.

2

Cub has fun at the pond.

Cub and Mom must rest.

7

Cub picks up a nut.

Mom can get the plant.

4

Mom has many nuts.

Mom bent.
Mom dug in the mud.

5

Strategic Intervention Decodable Reader 7

A Grand Plan

Written by Josh Grober

Illustrated by Ann Pierce

Phonics Skills

Digraphs sh, th	Sound of a as in ball, walk	
this	ball	all
fish	walk	call
with	talk	
trash	path	
that		
shack		
them		

Let us pick up the trash on the path.
That plan is good!

8

Let us catch this ball.

That is not my plan.

That is not fun at all.

Let us call Brad and Jim
and talk with them.

Let us catch a fish at that shack.

4

I can not walk to the shack and back.

5

Jane with Mom

Written by Peter Penn

Illustrated by Kim Renea

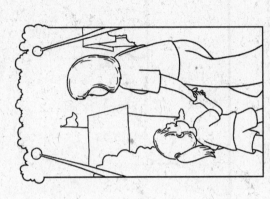

Phonics Skills

Long a (CVCe)		c/s/ and g/j/
Jane	make	ape	face
face	name	snake	cage
cage	cave	race	race
wave	gate	take	age

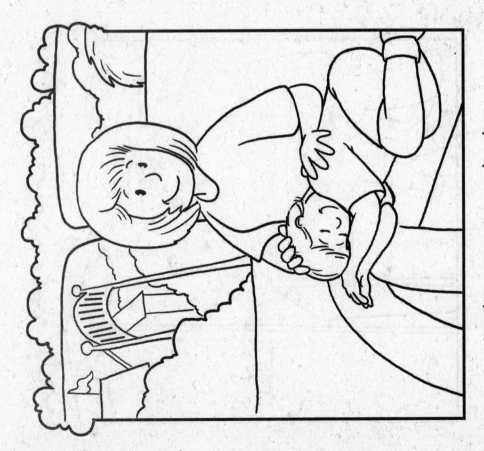

Jane can take a nap on the bus.

8

Jane can make an ape face.

Jane can wave at the gate.

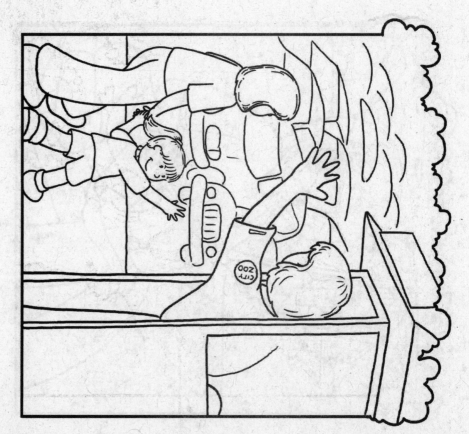

Jane can name the big cats.

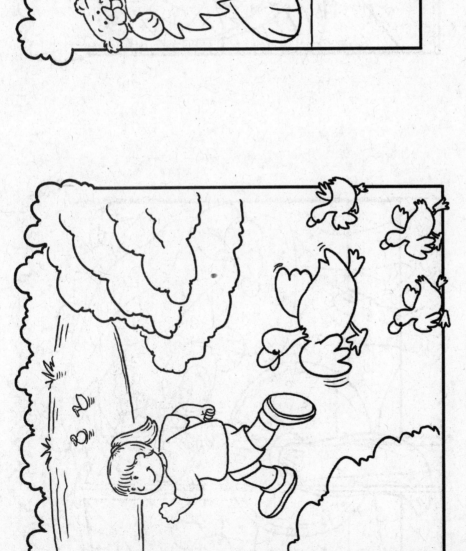

Jane can race with the ducks.
They can not run fast at this age.

6

Jane can talk like the snake
in that cage.

4

Jane can look in that cave.
A cub is in it.

5

We All Work

Written by Margaret Ronzarie

Illustrated by Dan Vick

Phonics Skills

Long i (CVCe)		Digraphs wh, ch, -tch	
like	ice	which	chop
rice	time	much	latch
		Chip	Champ
		chase	fetch

We did the jobs.
It is time for fun!

8

We all like to work.
Which jobs can we do?

2

Champ can chase and fetch.

7

Peg can make ice.

3

Chip can place trash
in sacks and take it out.

Dad can chop and mix.
Dad made too much rice.

Mom can fix this latch.

**Strategic Intervention
Decodable Reader 10**

Time to Swim

Written by Chris Arvetis

Illustrated by Sandra Camp

Phonics Skills

Long o (CVCe)		Contractions n't, 'm, 'll	
woke	hope	it'll	I'm
drove	hole	isn't	didn't
close	those		

It is fun at the lake.

Jim woke up.
"I hope it'll get hot."

"Do not wade close to those rocks,"
Mom calls.

"Can Tim and Rob come with us?
I'm calling them."

"We came to swim, didn't we?"
asks Rob.

Mom drove us to the lake.

Jim and Tim dig.
This hole isn't big yet.

Strategic Intervention
Decodable Reader 11

Can We Have Fun?

Written by John Roberts
Illustrated by Dan Vick

Phonics Skills

Long u (CVCe)	Long e (CVCe)	Inflected Ending -ed
June cube cute	Zeke	asked
Luke tune flute	these	named
rules		

Luke, June, and Zeke
had fun!

8

"Can June make a cube?"
Zeke asked.

Zeke did find these rules
under his box.

June made a cube.
June has a cute cube.

Luke asked, "Can Zeke
find game rules?"

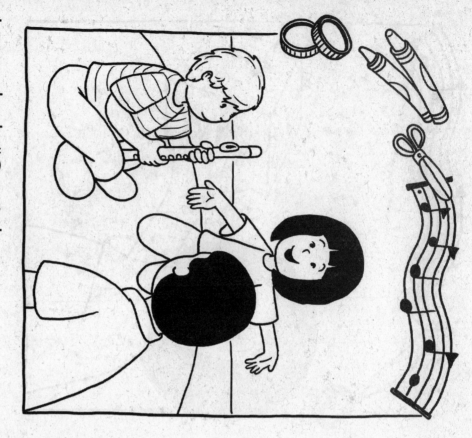

June asked, "Can Luke name a tune?"

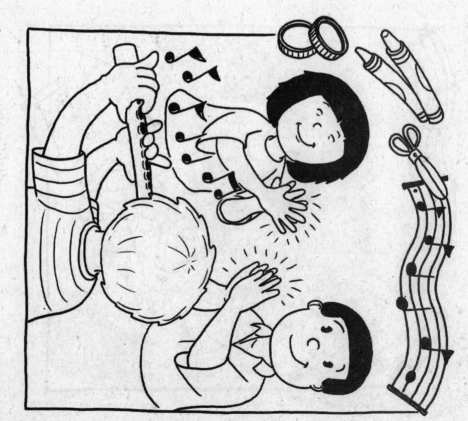

Luke named a tune.
It was a flute tune.

Dee Has Pets

Written by Dorothy Johnson
Illustrated by Kris Stanton

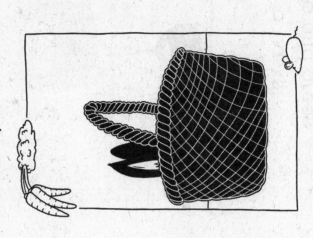

Phonics Skills

Long e: e, ee		Syllables VCCV
Dee	deep	green	basket	rabbit
keeps	she	feet	kitten
sweet	he	be

Dee has nice pets.
They like their home.

8

Dee has a basket.
It is deep and green.

Kitten likes to be with Rabbit.

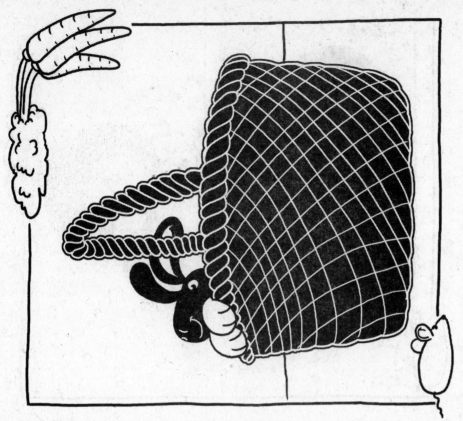

Dee keeps a small rabbit
in this basket.

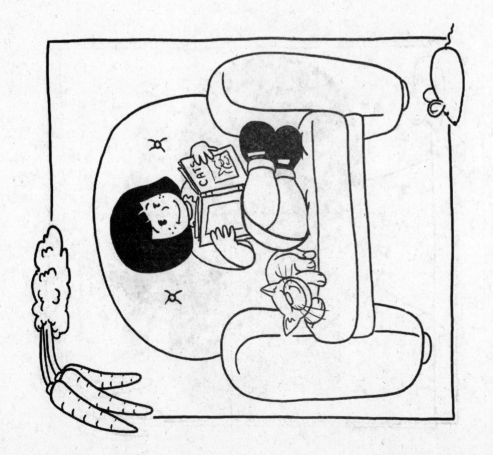

Dee also has a kitten.
He is tan.

Rabbit is black, but she
has white feet.

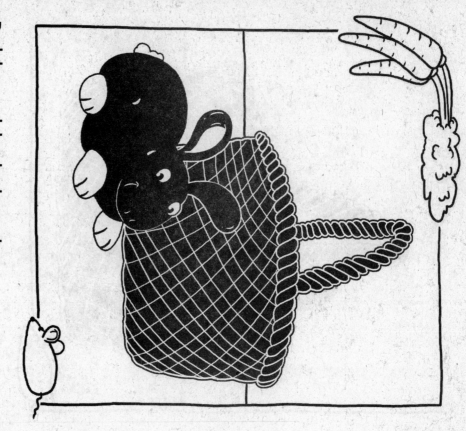

4

Rabbit is a sweet pet.
Dee likes her.

5

A Fishing Trip

Written by Dylan Demastri
Illustrated by Jeff Hann

Phonics Skills

Vowel Sounds of y: Long i, Long e		Long Vowel Pattern CV: as in me, hi, go		
Jenny	Ty	Bo	go	hi
try	funny	be	we	he
fry	tummy			
	my			

Ty rubs his tummy and he thinks of the fish fry.

8

Jenny, Ty, and Bo
will go fishing.
They came to my home.

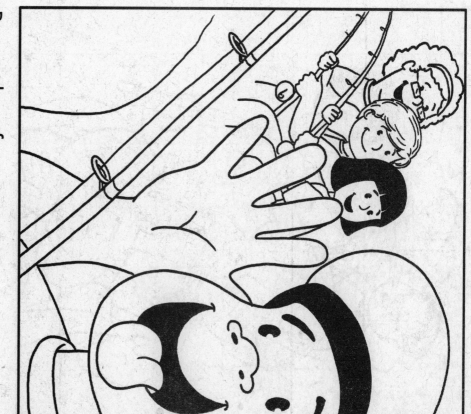

Bo made a funny
face as he fished.
"I got a fish!"

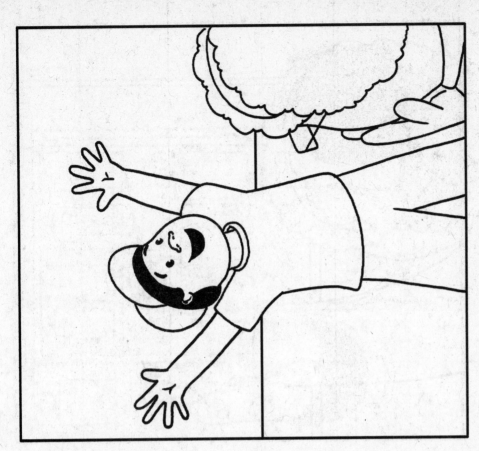

"Hi, Gwen," yelled Bo.
"We will try to
catch lots of fish."

We got poles and
Ty packed his bag.

"Will you be fishing all day?" I asked.

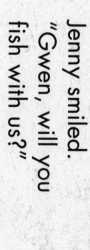

Jenny smiled. "Gwen, will you fish with us?"

What to Do

Written by Sally Hinkley

Illustrated by Dan Vick

Phonics Skills

Compound Words	Consonant Blends -ng, -nk	
pancakes	rang	drank
milkshakes	sink	things
catfish	long	think
everyone	trunk	hang
outside		
inside		

We go inside.
We hang up the hats.

Ben made pancakes for everyone.
We like pancakes.

We stand by the lake.
No catfish swam by.

The bell rang on the stove.
Ben gave us hot pancakes.

We think we need snug hats.
We see hats in that trunk.

We drank milkshakes.
We ate and then placed the
cups and plates in the sink.

4

Then we wanted new things to try.
We will take a long walk outside.

5

**Strategic Intervention
Decodable Reader 15**

Going to the Shore

Written by Peter Mok

Illustrated by Lisa Gilbert

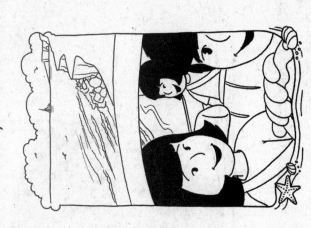

Phonics Skills

Adding -es	R-controlled or, ore	
tosses	catches	shore	for
glasses	dishes	short	more
boxes		or	

It is fun to go away.

Dad tosses a very big ball.
Lin catches it.

Dad closes the trunk.
We get in the car.

We can use it at the shore.
We are going for a short trip.

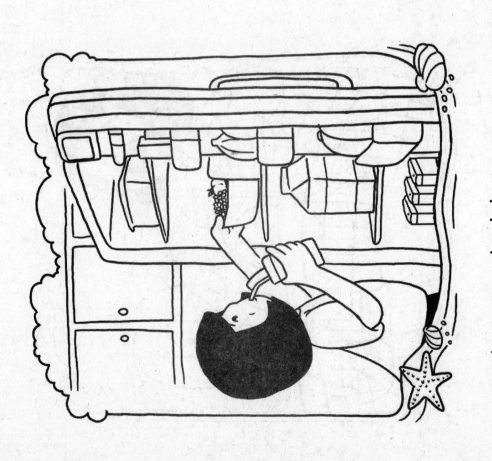

I can take more drink boxes.
I can pick plums or grapes
for my snack.

My bag is packed.
I can't close it.

4

Mom packs glasses and dishes.
We need them at the shore.

5

Jogging Time

Written by Bill Wright

Illustrated by Janice Perales

Phonics Skills

Inflected Endings -ed, -ing		R-controlled ar	
jogging	jogged	park	farm
falling	stopped	dark	star(s)
napping		cars	

We like jogging.
We will jog again, but
now we are napping.

8

We like to jog.
It makes us feel fine.

We go jogging in a race.
The cars stopped for the race.
We jogged and jogged.

We go jogging in the park.
We jogged and jogged in the park.

It is too dark to go jogging.
We see stars in the sky.
One star is falling.

We go jogging at the farm.
We jogged and jogged at the farm.

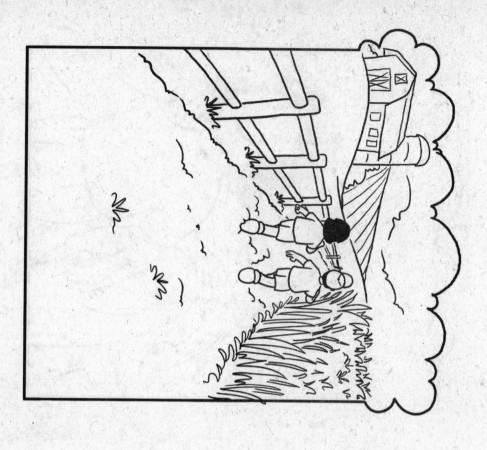

4

We go jogging around the track.
We jogged and jogged
around the track.

5

**Strategic Intervention
Decodable Reader 17**

Jane Takes Her Turn

Written by Karen Finch

Illustrated by Sam Loew

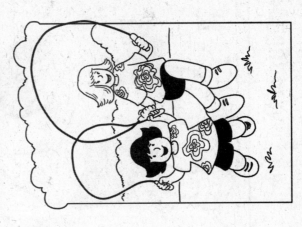

Phonics Skills

R-controlled er, ir, ur		Contractions 's, 've, 're	
girl	shirt(s)	first	she's	they're
stirs	stirring	her	it's	we've
turn	twirls	swirls		

Look at those swirls!
"We've made cute shirts,"
Jane said.

8

Jane visits Peg.
She's a nice girl.
Peg makes art.

"Wait," called Peg.
"It's not done.
Push it back in!"

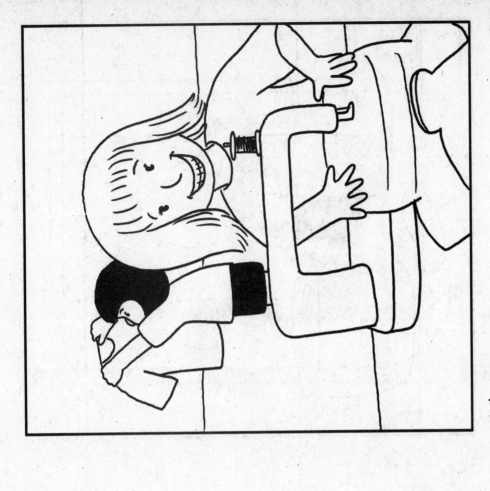

What art can
Jane make with Peg?
They're going to make fun shirts.

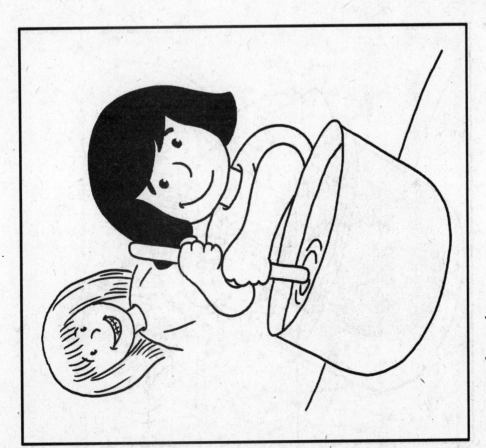

Jane takes her turn.
Jane twirls her shirt
in the pot with a stick.

First, Peg stirs
in the pink pot.
She's stirring it well.

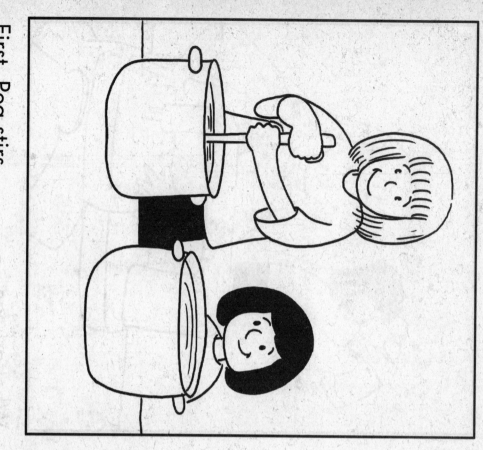

Next, Peg stirs
in the green pot.
Peg makes her shirt.

Penny Wins First Prize!

Written by Bill Nieder
Illustrated by Lisa Key

That fudge cake is best.
It wins first prize!

8

There is a prize
for the best cake.
Does Penny like to bake?

2

"Did you make this cake?"
asked the judge.
"It is the biggest cake."

7

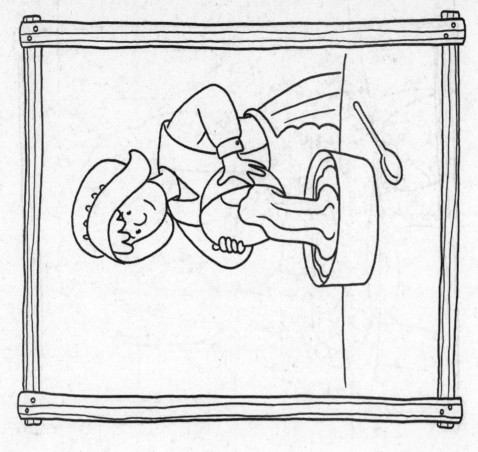

Penny will bake a cake
to win that prize.
She mixes faster and faster.

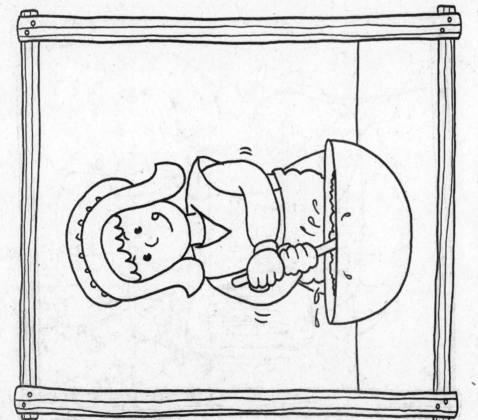

"I will try again," said Penny.
She did not mix as fast.
She added fudge.

Her cake is flat.
"This cake is the flattest.
It won't win."

She made her pan hotter.
Her cake burned.

Jay's Mail Day!

Written by Kelley South
Illustrated by Tom Amet

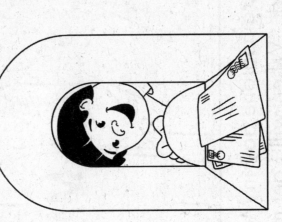

Phonics Skills

Long a: ai, ay			Possessives	
rained	day	May	mailman's	Jay's
Jay	mail	mailman	Mom's	
rain	train			

Jay,
This is your
first mail.
Jay is lucky!

Mom

When it rained one day in May,
Jay asked, "When will I get mail?"

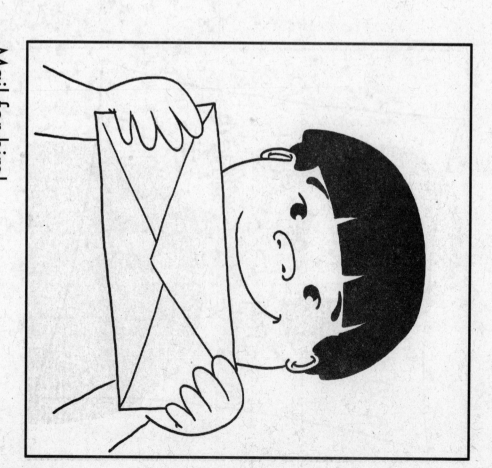

Mail for him!
Jay's mail makes him smile.
This is a happy day!

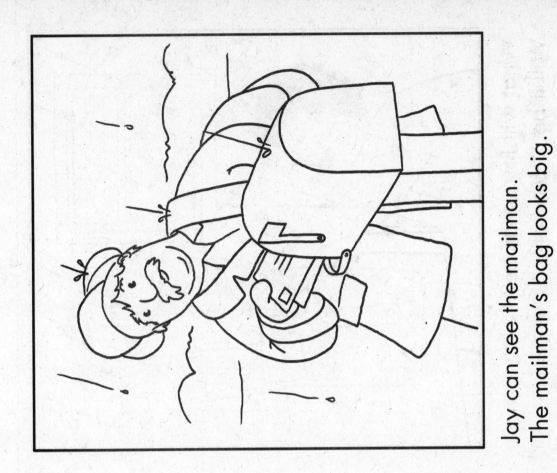

Jay can see the mailman.
The mailman's bag looks big.

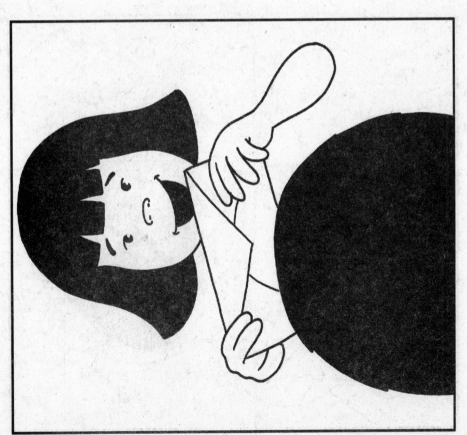

"Is that mail for me?" Jay asked.
"This note is for Jay," said Mom.

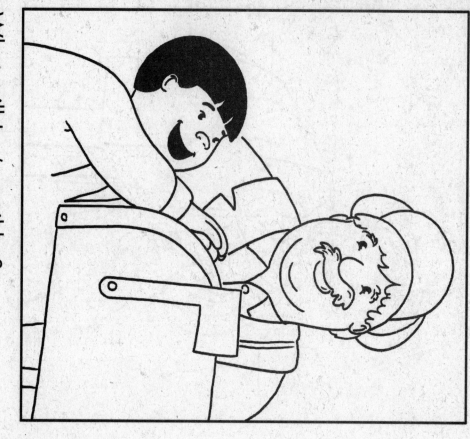

What will Jay's mail be?
Will it be a rain hat?
Will it be a small train?

Jay said "hi" to the mailman.
Some mail has Mom's name on it.
Jay takes the mail to Mom.

A Day at the Park

Written by Anita Flores

Illustrated by George Lynn

Phonics Skills

Long e: ea		Inflected Endings	
Jean	neat	cried	tried
treat	team	dried	
leaf	dream		

At last this fun day was over.

"Such a nice day!" Jean cried.

"It seemed like a dream."

Jean and Tom went to this park.
This park seemed nice.
Signs at the gates said
"Keep this park neat."

At the lake,
Jean and Tom got
to feed ducks
and see big fish.

"We will treat it well so that we can enjoy it again," Tom noted.

Then Tom drew on his art pad. Jean tried to draw a dried leaf. She made it look nice.

"Look at these trees!"
Jean cried.
"Colors like these can be
a nice treat."

4

Tom asked Jean,
"Can we play with that team?"
They played three games.

5

Toad's Big Plan

Written by Renée McLean
Illustrated by Alex Bream

Phonics Skills

Long o: oa, ow				Consonant Blends (CCCV)	
Toad	pillow	loaf		scrap	sprang
row	boat	follow		sprinted	spring
snow	coat	road			

Toad stuck the map
in his coat.
He went down the road
to his snug home.

8

Toad found a scrap.
It was a map.
He made a wild plan.
"I must see Bird at once!" he cried.

2

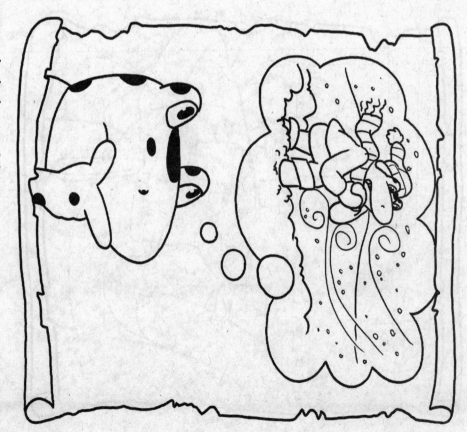

Toad did not like snow.
"That is smart," said Toad.
"We will go this spring."

7

Toad sprang up.
He packed his pillow
and a hot loaf.

"But, Toad," said Bird,
"I have jobs at home.
And snow may come soon."

He sprinted to Bird's home.
"Bird!" he yelled.
"Can you read this map?"

"We must row in that boat.
We must follow this map.
We will be rich!"

A Pie That Hits the Sky

Written by Kiran Smedley
Illustrated by Christopher Calvetti

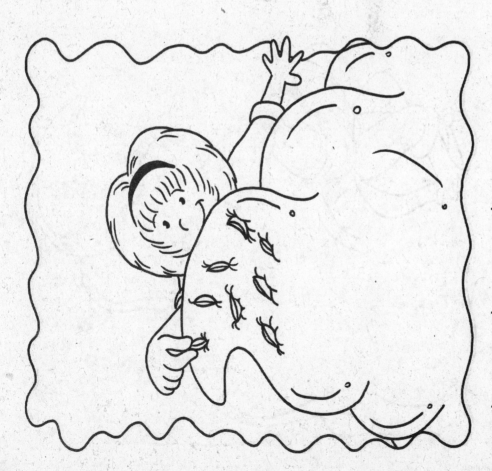

Barb put eight nuts right on top.
"That is how I like my pie,"
Barb said.

8

"I will make my pie,"
said Barb.
She wrote her list
of things to use.

2

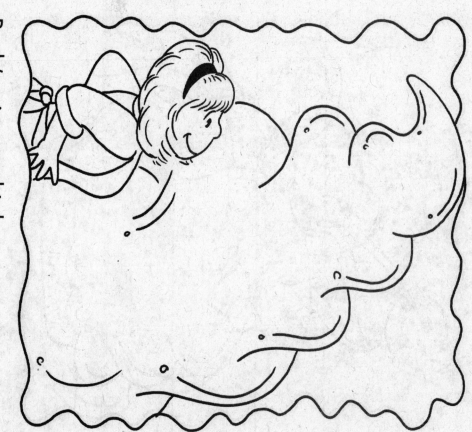

Barb's pie was high.
"It's not quite as high as the sky yet,"
Barb said with a laugh.

7

© Pearson Education

Barb got fresh peaches.
She cut the peaches
with her sharp knife.

Barb knows how to
make her pie big.
She piles sweet cream
on top of her pie.

6 3

"Bring me nice plums,"
called Barb.
"I will add them
to my pie."

4

We gave plums
for Barb's pie.
Barb's pie got bigger.

5

Zack at Bat

Written by Wes Long
Illustrated by Jill Vander

Phonics Skills

Compound Words		Vowel Patterns ew, ue, ui		
baseball	inside	Blue	Crew	flew
ballpark	newsstand	cruise	newsstand	

Zack stops at the newsstand
the next day.
His picture is in the paper.
Zack is a baseball star!

This is a big baseball game
for the Blue Crew.
Will the team be the champs?

2

That is Zack's first hit!
The Blue Crew wins.
They are the champs!

7

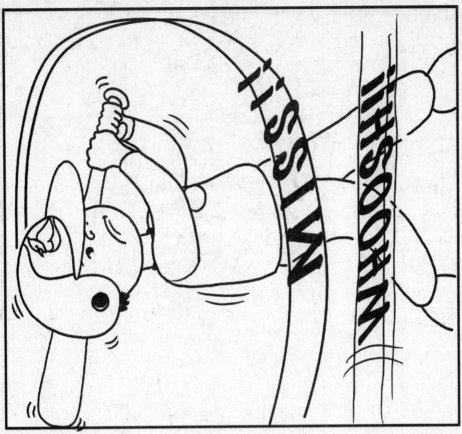

It is Zack's last turn at bat.
He swings. He misses.
He swings again. He misses.

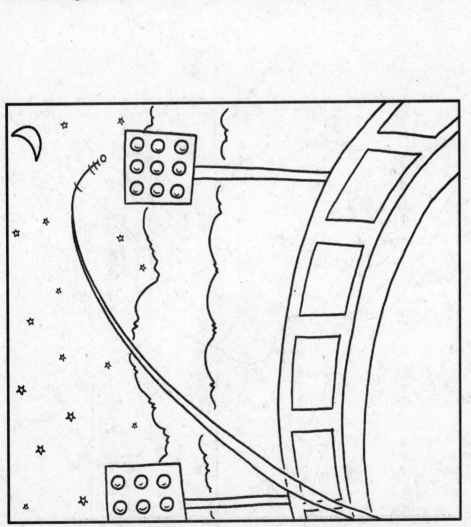

3

That ball is not
inside the ballpark.
That ball flew
above tall trees.

Will Zack get a hit?
Will Zack cruise the bases?
He grips his bat.
Zack swings hard. Crack!

Dads and moms jump up.
Where did that ball go?

The Spaceship

Written by Reonne Reed
Illustrated by Ted Corpell

Phonics Skills

Suffixes -ly, -ful	Vowels oo as in moon
quickly safely	Moon. tools
hopeful sadly	food too
	room

The big spaceship did not start.
"Oh, well," Dan said sadly.
"We can try again."

8

Kim and Dan made a plan.
They will go up to the Moon!

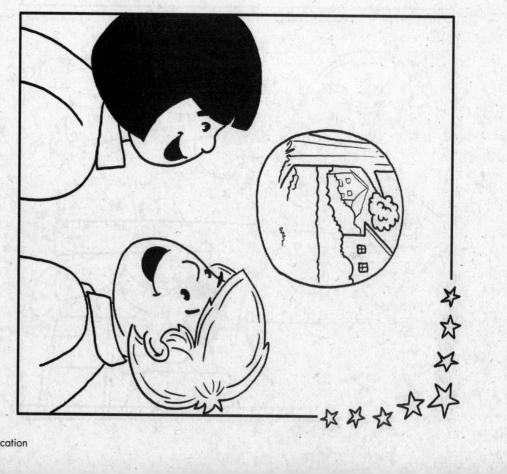

Kim and Dan got in.
It had lots of room.
Dan was hopeful.

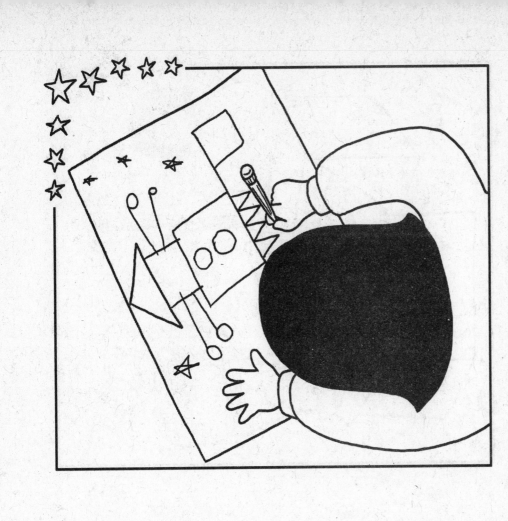

"Can we get there?" Kim asked.
"We will need a big spaceship."

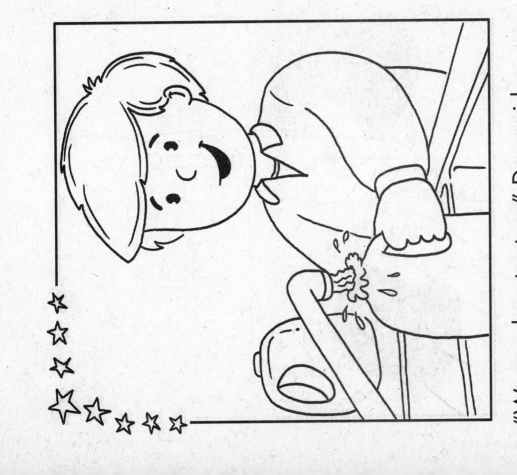

"We need water too," Dan said.
He filled his jug.
He got a jug for Kim too.

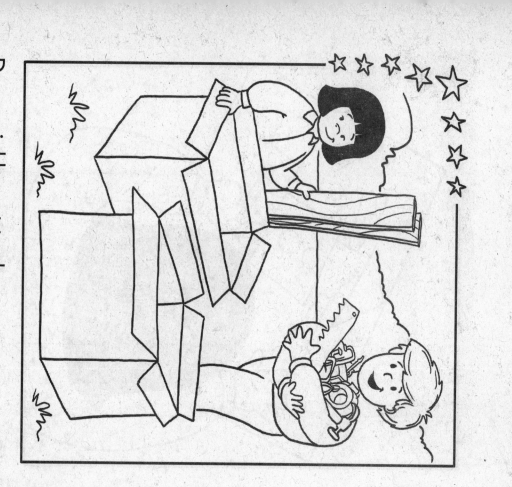

Dan quickly got tools.
"Use those tools safely,"
he said.

4

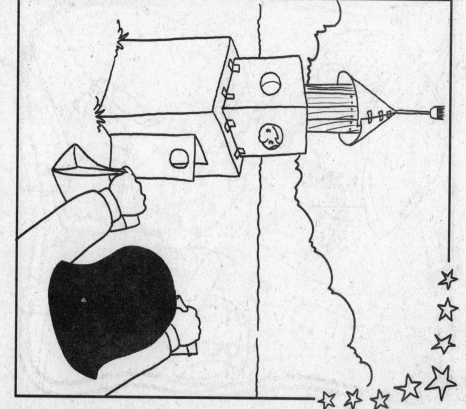

When they made the ship,
Kim got food for them.
"Is this all we need?" she asked.

5

Race Day

Written by Stacey Adams
Illustrated by Hal Bing

Phonics Skills

Vowel Diphthong ow/ou/	Consonant + le	
brown	down	gobble	little
now	crowd	stumble	
town	how		

How fast Sam runs!
He must not stumble.
Sam is first!
This is a great day for Sam.

8

This is Sam's big day.
He jumps out of his bed.

Sam starts running.
He is fast.
He remembers what
Mom and Dad said.

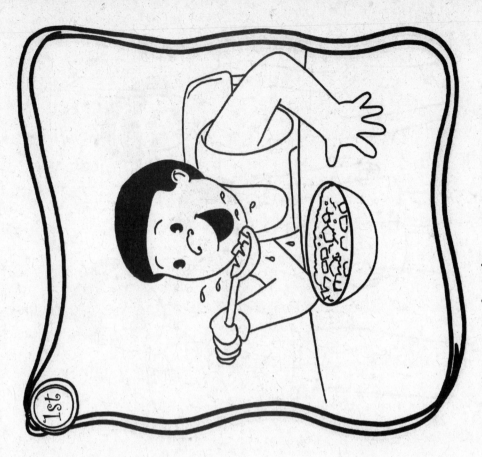

Sam has on his brown pants.
He runs down to eat.
He tries to gobble down his food.
He cannot sit still.

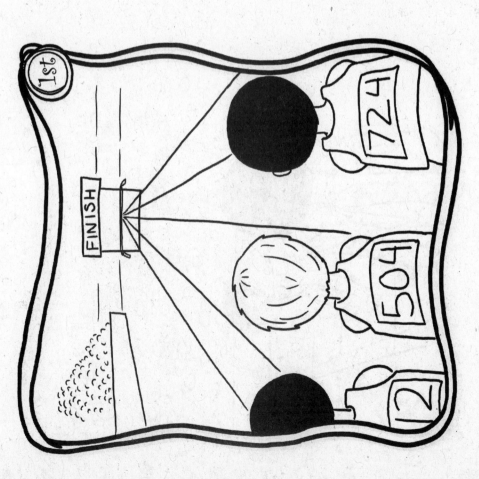

Sam gets in line.
He sees the tape far away.
He must get there first.

He and his mom and dad
go to the track.
Mom and Dad tell him
to do his best.

4

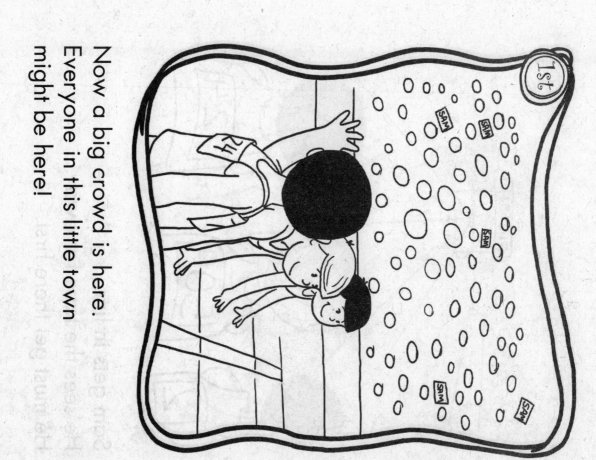

Now a big crowd is here.
Everyone in this little town
might be here!

5

**Strategic Intervention
Decodable Reader 26**

Time for Bed

Written by Leslie Lin
Illustrated by Ben Guff

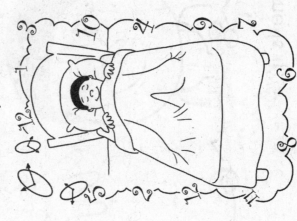

Phonics Skills

Vowel Diphthong ou/ou/		Syllable VCV	
mouth	count	silent	opened
found	couch	began	even
shout	loud		

Ted's lids drooped even more.
"It's time to close my eyes,"
said Ted.
He went to sleep.

8

"What time is it?"
asked Mom.
Ted was silent.

Ted was sleepy.
"It's time for bed," he said.
Mom nodded.

"Is it time to eat?" asked Ted.
Ted opened his mouth.
"No, it's not time to eat,"
said Mom.

"Is it time to shout?" asked Ted.
Ted began to be loud.
"No, it's not time to shout,"
said Mom.

"Is it time to count?"
asked Ted.
"No, it's not time to count,"
said Mom.

"Is it time to hide
and be found?" asked Ted.
Ted hid behind the couch.
"No, it's not time to hide," said Mom.

Strategic Intervention
Decodable Reader 27

The Cleaning Game

Written by Sarah Park
Illustrated by Elliott Jones

Phonics Skills

Vowels oo as in book		Inflected Endings -s, -es, -ed, -ing		
looks	good	goes	looks	finished	cleaning
books	took	starting	raced	joked	hiding
look		liked	racing	played	smiling
		asked			

"Can you play another cleaning game next week?" Danny asked.

8

Emmy goes to see Danny.
Danny looks sad.
"I cannot play,"
Danny said sadly.

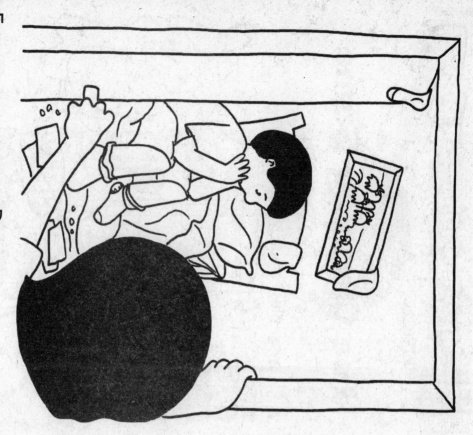

Danny's mom took a look.
"Good job!" she said.
"We played all day!"
Emmy said, smiling.

"None of my chores
got finished this week."
"We can still play," Emmy said.

Emmy found lost books
hiding in Danny's big trunk.
Danny found a hat he liked.
He found racing cars with his blocks.

"We can make cleaning a game!
This is a good starting place."
Emmy and Danny
raced to pick things up.

4

They joked about
Danny's messy ways.
Cleaning was fun
instead of dull.

5

Sue's Family Tree

Written by Howard Price
Illustrated by Bernard Cup

Phonics Skills

Vowel Diphthong oi, oy		Suffixes -er, -or	
joy	toy(s)	writer	actor
boys	soil	baker	farmer

Sue made her family tree.
She showed all these facts.
Sue is proud
of her family!

8

Today Sue must make
a family tree.
A family tree shows
who is in her family.

2

Dad's dad was a farmer.
He made things grow
in heavy, brown soil.

7

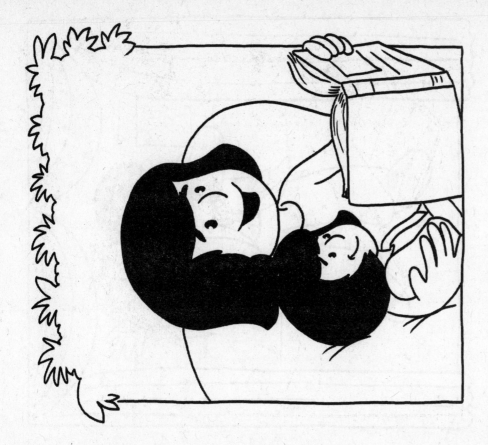

Sue starts with her mom.
Mom is a writer.
She writes books.
Sue likes her mom's books.

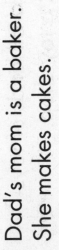

Dad's mom is a baker.
She makes cakes.

Sue's dad is an actor.
He acts with much joy.
Sue's dad is a good actor.

Mom's dad made all kinds of toys.
Mom's mom ran a toy shop.
Girls and boys liked
to see those nice toys.

Back to School

Written by Kevin Culler

Illustrated by Beth Hana

Phonics Skills

Vowel aw, au as in saw, auto

yawned   saw

lawns   draw

Short e: ea

ready

head

SCHOOL

Pat loves school!

He used his head.

He did so much.

He had the best day!

8

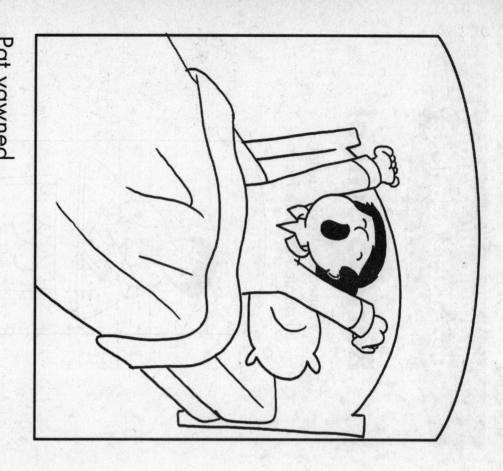

Pat yawned.
The day is starting!
It is Pat's big day.
He is ready for school.

2

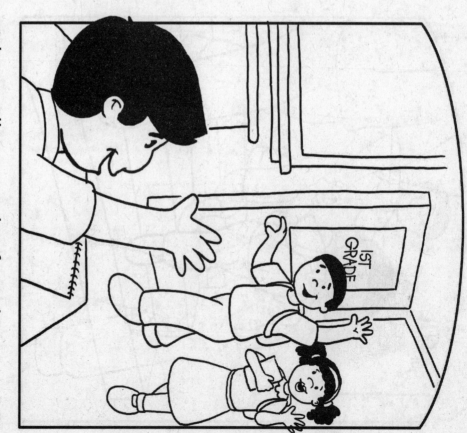

When will Pat see his friends?
There they are! Pat waved.
His friends waved back.
Pat is happy to be at school.

7

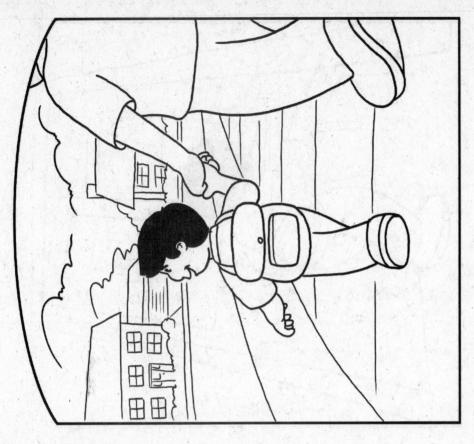

Pat walked with Dad.
He saw trees and lawns.
He saw homes and shops.
Will they be there soon?

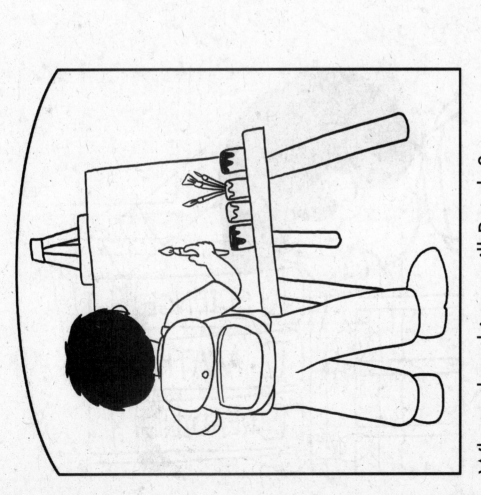

What other things will Pat do?
Will he draw?
Will he paint?
Will he sing?

Pat got to his classroom first.
Pat is ready to sit down.
How will he use his head?

1ST GRADE

Pat will study science.
He will study math.
He will study many things.

SCIENCE

MATH

READING

Strategic Intervention Decodable Reader 30

Lost Bird

Written by Jane Marks

Illustrated by Jim Burg

Phonics Skills

Prefixes un-, re-	Long Vowel Patterns	
	old	cold
	find	kind
unhappy refilled	mind	

The three birds smiled.
"We are kind.
We do not mind."

8

Dee is a small bird.
She plays in the woods.
She went to different parts
of the woods. She got lost.

2

Those birds helped Dee
find her way home.
"You are kind," said Dee's mom.

7

Dee felt unhappy.
She had no water.
She did not carry much food.
Dee sat down and cried.

The birds took Dee
to a cold stream.
The birds refilled her bottle
and gave her bread.

Three birds came.
"Did you get lost?"
asked the one old bird.

4

"Yes," she answered.
"I am lost,
and my bottle is dry."

5